DATE DUE			

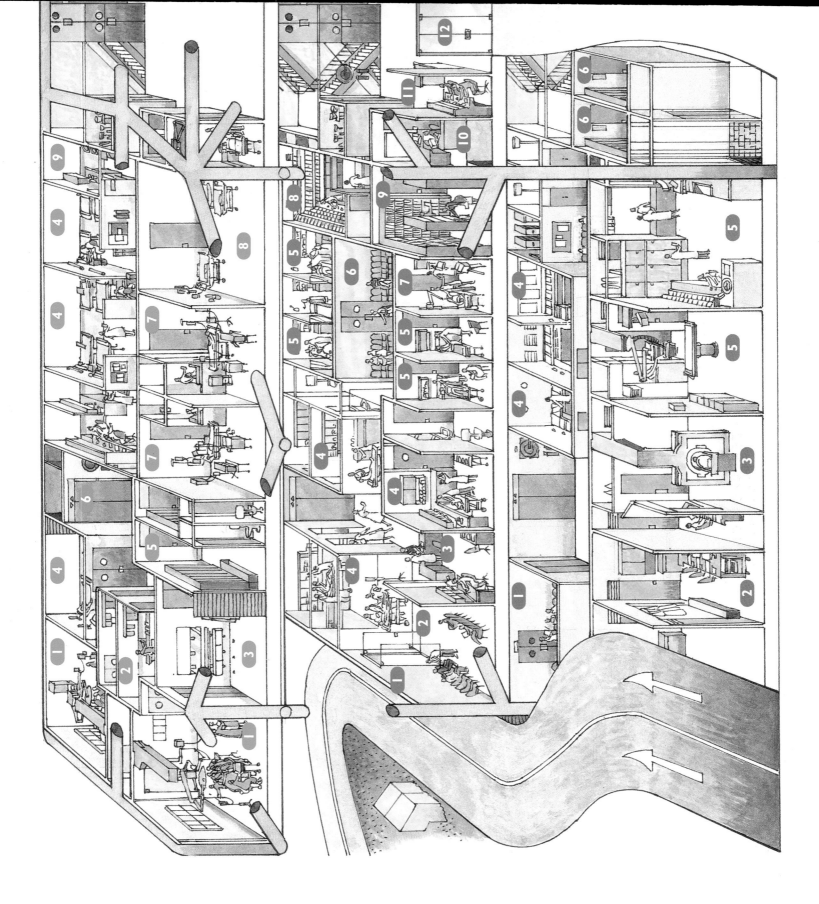

First floor

1 Operating rooms
Surgeons perform operations in this part of the hospital.

2 Anesthesiologists' room
In this room, anesthesiologists prepare drugs and gasses for making patients unconscious.

3 Scrub room
Medical staff wash with antiseptics here to kill germs on their bodies.

4 Surgical floors
Patients stay here before and after operations.

5 Locker room
Before operations, doctors and surgeons change into their gowns and masks here.

6 Elevators
Elevators take patients to and from the operating rooms.

7 Intensive care
Seriously ill patients are monitored 24 hours a day here.

8 Recovery room
Patients come here to wake up after operations.

9 Utility room
Dirty sheets, clothing and trash bags are collected in this room.

10 Main elevators
These carry people, carts and equipment between floors.

11 Medical floors
Patients here are treated mainly with medicine. One unit is for women, the other is for men.

12 Delivery rooms
Obstetricians and nurses help women as they give birth here.

13 Neonatal unit
Ill or premature babies are monitored here, until they are well enough to go home.

14 Day room
Pregnant women and new mothers come here to relax.

15 Maternity floor
Pregnant women and new mothers stay in this ward.

16 Staff room
Hospital staff can come here to relax, eat or watch television.

17 Play area

18 Pediatric floor
Sick children are cared for here. Boys and girls stay together on the same floor.

tal

ome are new and
eneral hospitals
pecialist hospitals
s. This picture
e building is
t happens in
d the rooms
ach room,
e.

y the color
ment by red.
he colors
w which floor
eading about,
e is a simplified

BUILDING WORKS

HOSPITAL

John Malam

PETER BEDRICK BOOKS

CONTENTS

The fold-out section at the start of this book shows the main hospital building from the outside. Open it up to reveal a cutaway view of the inside, with a key to what happens in each room. After this you will find a plan of the hospital grounds.

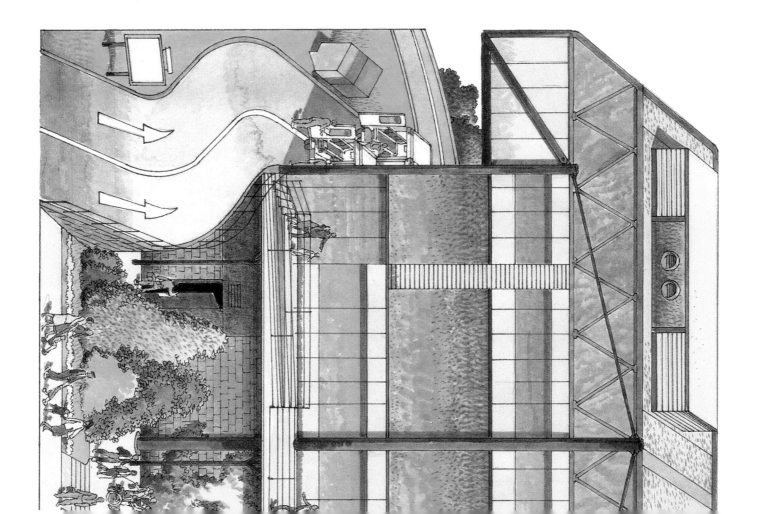

Ground floor

1 Entrance to the emergency room
Ambulances arrive here with seriously ill and injured patients.

2 Waiting area

3 Reception desk
Patients report here on arrival.

4 Treatment rooms
Emergency patients receive treatment here.

5 Outpatient department
Doctors advise and treat outpatients in these rooms.

6 Waiting area

7 Ultrasound room
Pregnant women have ultrasound scans here to check that their babies are healthy.

8 Pharmacy
Pharmacists prepare drugs and medications here.

9 Patient record office
In this room patients' medical records are stored.

10 Admissions office
Patients' names and addresses are kept here.

11 Switchboard
Telephone operators answer phone calls to the hospital in this room.

12 Main entrance

13 Information board

14 Gift shop
The gift shop sells newspapers, magazines, food and flowers.

15 Security office
Here security guards watch what happens in the hospital on video screens.

16 Staff room
Hospital staff can come here to relax, eat or watch television.

17 Quiet room
Patients and visitors come here to pray or to sit quietly.

18 Cafeteria
Visitors can have a drink and a snack here.

19 Waiting area

20 Dietician's office
The dietician works out special eating plans for patients.

21 Physical therapy
Physical therapists work out exercise programs and treat patients in this part of the hospital.

22 Restrooms

23 Technicians' room
A room for the hospital technicians to relax.

Basement

1 Waiting room

2 Radiology
Radiologists examine CT scans on computer screens in this area.

3 CT scanner
This scanner shows cross sections through the human body.

4 Viewing rooms
Doctors and radiologists look at x-ray images here.

5 X-ray rooms
X-ray pictures are taken and developed in here.

6 Storage rooms

7 Waiting area

8 Staff cafeteria
Hospital staff eat their meals here.

9 Kitchens
Cooks prepare meals for staff and patients in the kitchens.

10 Laundry
Dirty sheets, clothes and towels are washed, ironed and folded in these rooms.

11 Reception area

12 Managers' offices
The hospital managers make sure that the building runs smoothly and efficiently.

13 Pathology
In these high tech laboratories scientists examine blood and tissue samples.

14 MRI scanning room
In this room magnetic resonance imaging (MRI) scanners use electromagnetic forces to make images of the human body.

15 X-ray room
X-ray pictures are taken and developed in here.

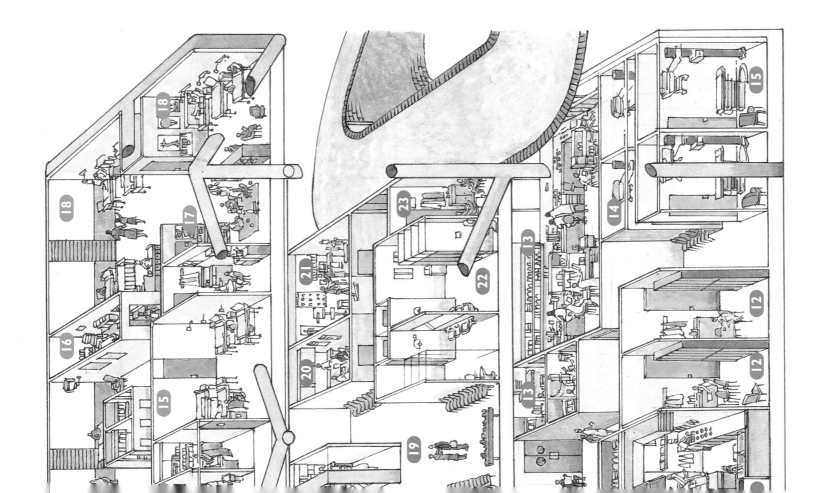

What is a hospital?

A hospital is a place for treating sick people. It is where doctors, nurses and many other people work. A large general hospital contains the machines and medicine needed to treat almost every kind of illness or injury. A specialist hospital is often smaller, and concentrates on treating one particular disease or condition.

There are hundreds of rooms inside a hospital. In many of them patients are treated and medical staff work. There are many more rooms where patients or their visitors do not go, but which are essential to the successful working of the hospital.

Some departments, such as emergenc front or side of the building for a very g Sick and injured people can be brought front doors, both by emergency vehicles are given immediate life-saving treatmen room, so it must be easy to reach. Matern the front entrance, because women abou to be able to get to the department as qu

Departments at the back of the build are often not for the treatment of patient as vital as that of the floors and operating and laundry are in the basement, away fro Delivery vehicles come and go all day lo the way of emergency vehicles.

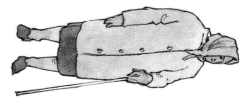

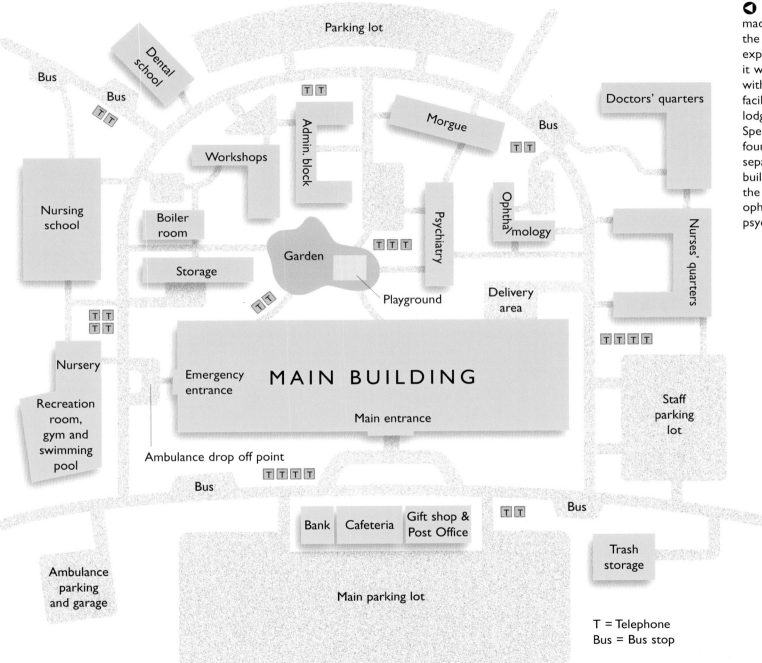

Parking lot

Dental school

Bus

Bus

T T T

Admin. block

T T

Morgue

Bus

T T

Doctors' quarters

Workshops

Nursing school

Boiler room

Ophtha/mology

Nurses' quarters

Psychiatry

T T T

Garden

Storage

T

Playground

Delivery area

T T T T

Nursery

MAIN BUILDING

Emergency entrance

Staff parking lot

Recreation room, gym and swimming pool

Main entrance

Ambulance drop off point

T T T T

Bus

Bus

T T

Bus

Ambulance parking and garage

Bank | Cafeteria | Gift shop & Post Office

Trash storage

Main parking lot

T = Telephone
Bus = Bus stop

◀ A modern hospital is made up of much more than the main block that you will explore in this book. In fact, it works as a small community with its own stores, recreation facilities, transportation, staff lodging and parking lots. Specialist departments are found in smaller blocks, separate from the main building. These may include the dental school (for teeth), ophthalmology (for eyes) and psychiatry (for mental health).

Emergency room

This is one of the busiest departments in the hospital, with patients arriving 24 hours a day, every day of the year. Some arrive by ambulance, while others make their own way.

As soon as patients arrive here, a triage nurse sees them. The French word *triage* is often used to describe the work of the assessment nurse. It means "sorting according to condition." The nurse finds out whether the patients have any allergies to medicines, whether they have been in the hospital before and, if they have had an accident, how it happened. The most seriously ill or injured patients are seen at once. Those with less urgent problems wait for treatment. Some may be advised to go home and see their family doctor instead.

After the patients have been assessed, they receive treatment for their conditions. Serious cases may be taken to intensive care, or into the operating room for an operation. Less serious cases, such as broken bones or minor cuts, are dealt with in the emergency room.

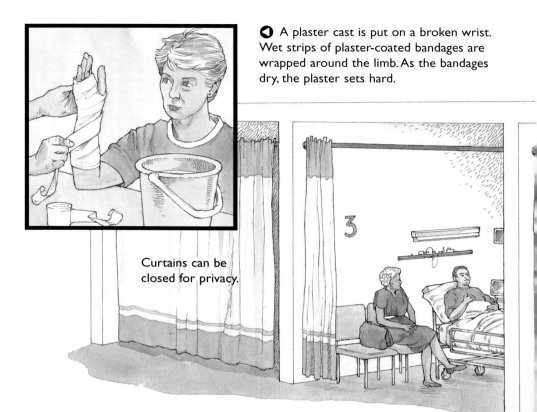

◁ A plaster cast is put on a broken wrist. Wet strips of plaster-coated bandages are wrapped around the limb. As the bandages dry, the plaster sets hard.

Curtains can be closed for privacy.

▶ A handheld video camera linked to a computer sends images of an x-ray to a hospital many miles away. There, a doctor views the x-ray picture on a computer and sends back advice about treatment. This is called telemedicine.

Some of the most urgent cases involve patients who have suffered a heart attack, been badly burned, or been involved in a major accident. These patients are almost always brought to the hospital by ambulance. Paramedics inside the ambulance begin to treat the patient during the journey to the hospital.

A patient with a broken bone is sent to the radiology department to have an x-ray. If it is a simple break, the patient goes to the fracture clinic, which is part of the emergency room. A plaster cast is put around the broken bone. If the break needs surgery, the patient may have an operation to insert metal pins, screws or plates to hold the bone in place. A plaster cast is put on afterwards.

Before patients leave the emergency room, they are told how to take care of themselves until they are fully recovered.

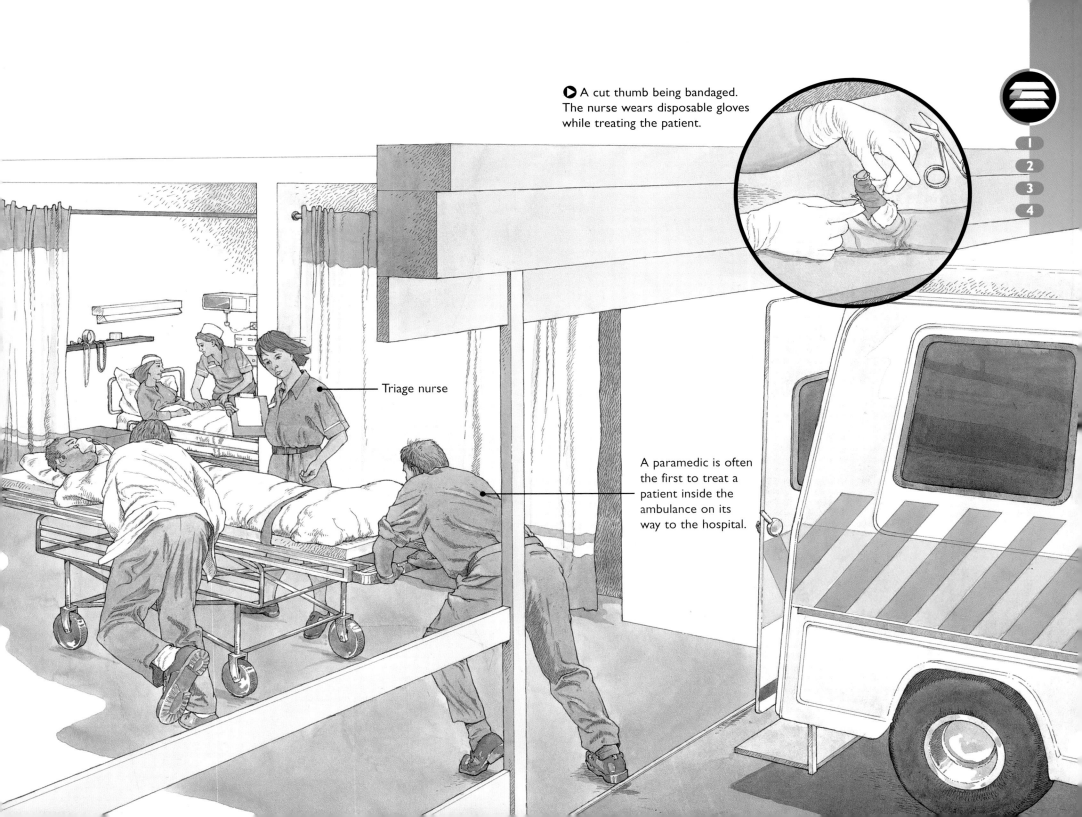

▶ A cut thumb being bandaged. The nurse wears disposable gloves while treating the patient.

Triage nurse

A paramedic is often the first to treat a patient inside the ambulance on its way to the hospital.

Outpatient

The outpatient department is one of the largest and busiest parts of the hospital. Outpatients are people who are well enough to stay out of the hospital, but who come in to one of its departments for treatment or a consultation.

The main part of the department is the waiting area. This is a large open room, where outpatients wait to be seen. They sit on chairs, read magazines, and buy snacks from the snack bar or gift shop.

Corridors lead away to all parts of the hospital. Clear signs point the way to different departments, so it is easy for patients to find their way around.

People come to the outpatient department for many different reasons. Some may have been patients on a medical/surgical floor, and although they have recovered enough to leave the hospital, they need to come back for checkups to make sure they are continuing to get better.

Others become outpatients if their family doctor advises them to go to the hospital for tests. For example, patients with ear, nose and throat problems usually go to a specialist clinic in the outpatient department.

Easy access for disabled people is important. For this reason the department is on the ground floor with no steps to climb. An elevator takes patients to clinics on other floors.

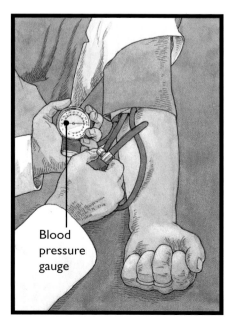

Blood pressure gauge

A shop sells newspapers, magazines, drinks and snacks.

◐ A patient's blood pressure is taken with an instrument called a sphygmomanometer. High blood pressure can be a sign of poor health.

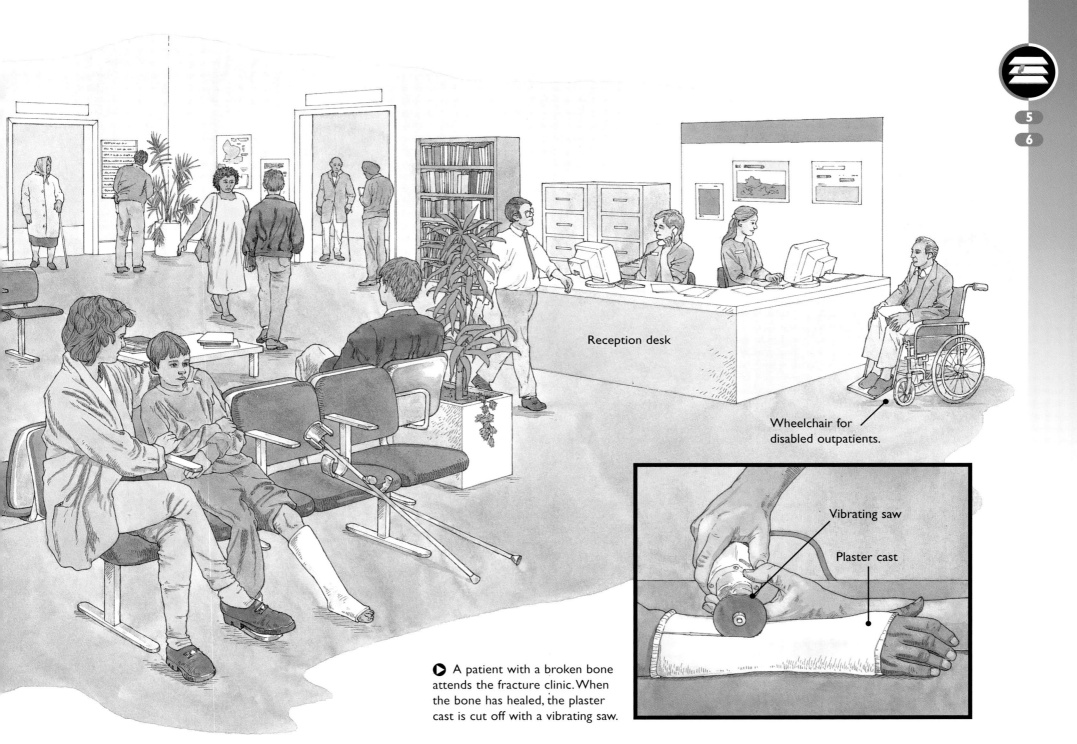

Reception desk

Wheelchair for disabled outpatients.

Vibrating saw

Plaster cast

▶ A patient with a broken bone attends the fracture clinic. When the bone has healed, the plaster cast is cut off with a vibrating saw.

Pharmacy

All medications used in the hospital are stored in the pharmacy. The people who work here are called pharmacists. They prepare medications for patients on the floors, and also for the outpatients.

The pharmacy is one of the secure areas of the hospital, which means that only specially-trained people are allowed to enter the department. This is because it contains drugs and medications that must be handled very carefully, often under controlled conditions.

Instructions for medications are called prescriptions. They are written by doctors and list the medications needed by a patient. Each prescription states the amount, or dose, to be taken.

A pharmacist keys the prescription details into a computer, which prints out a sticky label. On the label is the name of the patient, the name of the medication, and instructions about how and when to take it. One label is printed for each medication listed on the prescription.

Scientific books and magazines keep pharmacists up-to-date with news about medications.

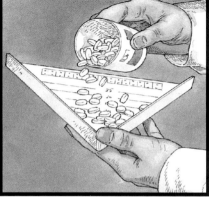

▲ Tablets are counted using a measuring tray called Pascal's triangle, or on special scales which weigh and count at the same time.

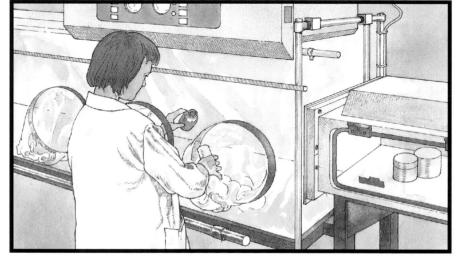

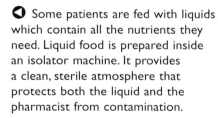

◀ Some patients are fed with liquids which contain all the nutrients they need. Liquid food is prepared inside an isolator machine. It provides a clean, sterile atmosphere that protects both the liquid and the pharmacist from contamination.

This gauge records the temperature inside the refrigerator.

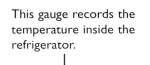 A pharmacist preparing medicine in a bowl called a mortar. It is being mixed with a grinder called a pestle.

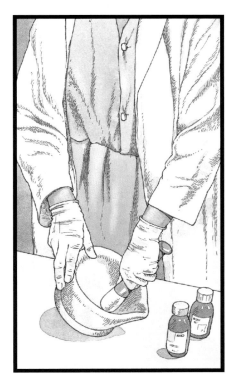

Around the pharmacy are shelves and cupboards filled with medical supplies, from which the pharmacist collects the medicines for each prescription. Certain medicines have to be kept at a cool temperature—these are stored in a large refrigerator until they are needed.

The pharmacist measures the amount of medicine to be put into each bottle, jar or box. The instruction labels are stuck on to these containers. Before medications leave the pharmacy, they are carefully checked to make sure no mistakes have been made.

The medications for use in the hospital are taken straight to the floors. Those for the outpatients go to the pharmacy, where they are picked up by the patient.

Physical therapy

Some patients need treatment to strengthen weak muscles. Others need help because they have stiff joints, or because they feel pain. All these problems can be treated by careful exercise, massage or heat. This type of treatment is called physical therapy, and people trained to do this work are physical therapists.

A patient recovering from an operation, or after a plaster cast has been removed from a broken limb, may need exercise to help their muscles get used to working again. Patients who suffer from arthritis, which makes their joints swollen and painful, come to physical therapy for massage and heat treatment. An athlete with a sprained muscle will come here too.

Physical therapists have many ways of improving patients' mobility and reducing pain. In a hydrotherapy room a patient is treated in a pool of warm water. The patient finds it easier to exercise, as the water supports their body weight. Regular exercise for short periods in water improves muscle strength, which helps the patient regain normal body movement. It also improves blood circulation and helps the patient to relax.

Patients with arthritis in their hands may be given heat treatment. This is often followed by massage, where the hands are gently stroked to help the joints regain movement.

Patients lift weights and exercise on stationary bicycles to strengthen their muscles.

Water in the pool is heated to around 98° fahrenheit.

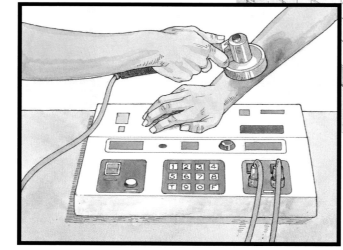

◀ An ultrasound machine sends sound waves into body tissues to reduce swelling and inflammation.

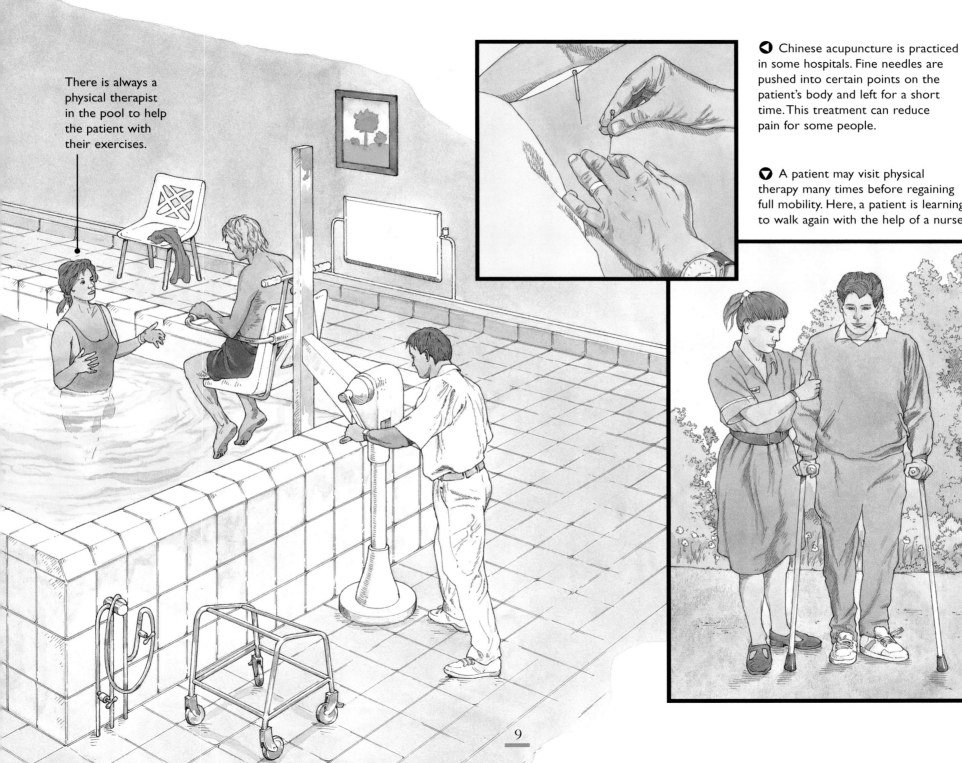

There is always a physical therapist in the pool to help the patient with their exercises.

◀ Chinese acupuncture is practiced in some hospitals. Fine needles are pushed into certain points on the patient's body and left for a short time. This treatment can reduce pain for some people.

▼ A patient may visit physical therapy many times before regaining full mobility. Here, a patient is learning to walk again with the help of a nurse.

Operating room

Most patients are brought to the operating room from a surgical floor, where they may have spent the night before their operation. But patients who have been in an accident, or who are suffering from a sudden illness, come straight here from the emergency room.

The operating room is near the surgery floor. Patients are transferred the short distance from the floor to the operating room by gurney. Patients are asked whether they have any allergies to medications, and if they have given permission for their operation to be performed. They are also asked when they last ate, as surgery can only be performed if the patient has not eaten for several hours.

Strong lights shine on the patient. They are movable, so the doctors and nurses have a clear view at all times.

Vital signs monitor

Every piece of equipment can be moved around the operating room.

Operating table

⬤ A patient's vital signs are monitored at all times. The colored lines on the screen show heart rate, blood pressure, breathing rate, and how much oxygen is in the blood.

From the waiting area the patient is wheeled into the anesthetic room. An adult patient is given an injection of anesthetic. A child is given a gas to breathe. Whichever is used, the patient quickly falls into a deep sleep. The anesthetic paralyses the muscles, so that the patient does not move during the operation. It also stops them from feeling any pain.

When they are in a deep sleep, the patient is transferred to the operating room. It is a "clean area"—everything is kept free from germs, including the air, which is cleaned before it comes into the room. The surgical team wears face masks, non-slip safety shoes, sterile gowns and gloves.

During the operation the patient is given a mixture of gasses to keep them asleep. A ventilator keeps the patient breathing, and all the time their vital signs are checked to make sure they are in good condition.

When the operation is over, the patient is taken to the recovery room where the anesthetic slowly wears off. The patient is taken back to the surgical floor, or sometimes to intensive care if they are still ill enough to need special treatment.

Straps keep the leg from moving during the operation.

⬤ The operation table can be raised and lowered, and various pieces of equipment can be attached to it for different operations. This patient has been prepared for a leg operation.

▶ An ophthalmic microscope is used during an eye operation. Both the surgeon and assistant surgeon can see through it at the same time. Other medical staff can follow the operation on a video monitor.

Intensive care

Patients who are seriously ill are cared for in intensive care. It is "intensive" because patients need a lot of treatment before they are well enough to be moved to a general medical floor.

Patients come to the intensive care unit if they are too ill to return to a medical floor after an operation. Some are transferred here from a medical/surgical floor because they have become very ill and need extra care. Others may have had a serious accident, or be suffering from a condition which puts their life in danger.

In the center or at one end of the floor is the nurses' desk, where a computer screen displays information about all the patients. Each patient's heart rate, blood pressure and breathing rate can be shown on the screen. The nurses don't need to visit a patient each time they want to check their vital signs. This means there are fewer people walking around the ward. The lighting is kept low to make it comfortable for the sleeping and resting patients.

There are always a lot of machines surrounding patients' beds in intensive care, but they may not all be turned on. They are there in case of an emergency, ready to be used right away.

Patients in intensive care are often kept on life support machines which carry out some of the body's functions. The machines support a patient's life until they are well enough for their body to take charge again. A ventilator keeps a patient's lungs breathing, and a dialysis machine performs the work of their kidneys.

◀ The resuscitation or crash cart contains everything needed in an emergency—medicines, needles, and breathing and feeding tubes. It can be wheeled quickly to a patient's bedside.

Resuscitation cart

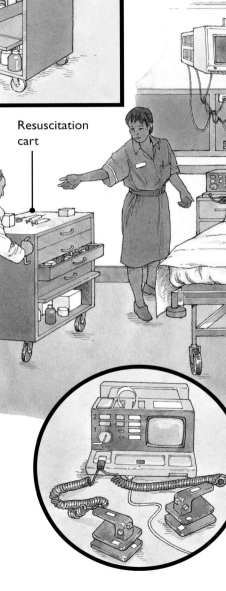

◀ If a patient's heart suddenly stops, or if it is not beating correctly, a defibrillator machine can restart it, or improve its beat. It gives a powerful electric shock through two paddles pressed on to the patient's chest.

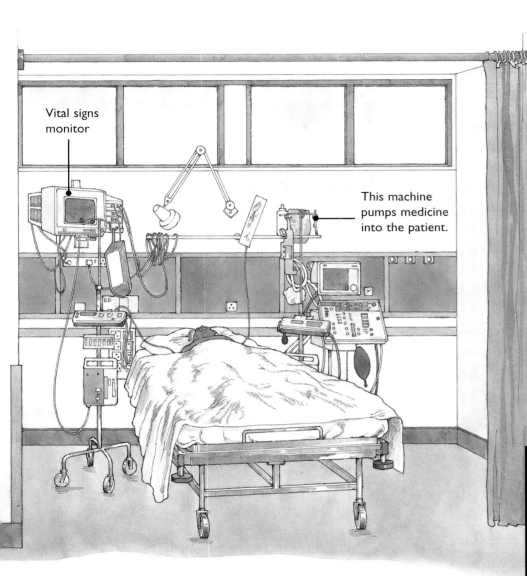

Vital signs
monitor

This machine
pumps medicine
into the patient.

▶ A blood gas analyzer checks
the levels of oxygen and carbon
dioxide in a patient's blood.
While in intensive care, patients
have their blood checked several
times a day to make sure their
condition is stable.

Medical/surgical floors

There are two types of nursing units in the hospital—the surgical floor and the medical floor. Patients go to the surgical unit to recover after an operation. The medical unit is for people who have not had surgery, but who are being treated with medications.

The length of time a patient stays on the surgical floor depends on the operation they have had. Patients recovering from major surgery, who may be seriously ill, might stay there for several weeks. These are long-term patients. Short-term patients may be kept in for only one or two nights. Some patients who leave the surgical unit may be well enough to go home. Others who are still ill may be moved to the medical unit, where treatment continues until they are fully recovered.

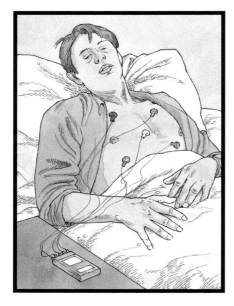

The beds on the surgical day unit are close together. A patient stays here only a short time.

◀ A patient with a heart condition on the medical floor may wear a telemetry transmitter. It monitors their heart rate and sends a signal to a computer on the nurses' desk.

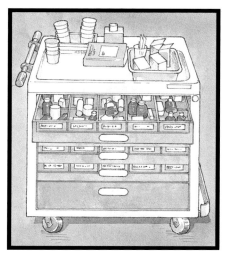

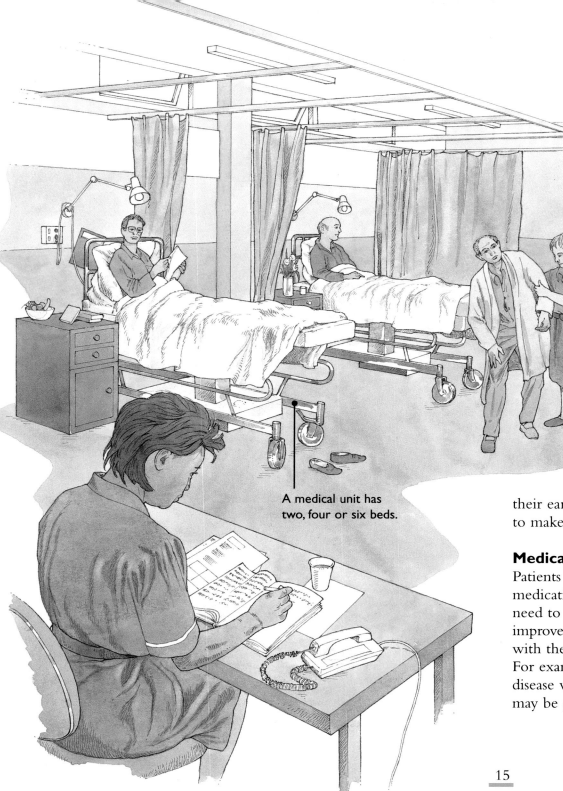

Each ward has a medicine cart, stocked with all the medications needed for the patients on the floor.

A medical unit has two, four or six beds.

The day unit is a separate part of the surgical floor, where patients have minor operations and go home on the same day. These operations often take only a short time to perform. Adults may have stitches taken out, or laser surgery for kidney and bladder stones. Children may have tubes inserted in their ears to improve hearing, or have infected adenoids removed to make breathing and speaking easier.

Medical floor

Patients on the medical floor are treated with medications. For some, medications cure them completely, and they stop taking them. Others need to take medications regularly, or must change their lifestyles to improve their health. In these cases, patients are taught how to live with their condition and control it once they leave the hospital. For example, a patient with diabetes learns how to control the disease with a medication or a change of a diet. Other patients may be given advice about doing regular exercise.

Pediatric floor

Children and adults stay on separate floors. The children's floor is a bright and cheerful place, with books to read, toys to play with, and pictures on the walls. Children are admitted to this floor from very young to age 16. After the age of 16 they are old enough to go to a floor for adults.

Children have their own special team of doctors and nurses to care for them. They give "pediatric" care to their young patients. Pediatric means the study of children and their diseases.

For many children, a stay in the hospital is often their first time away from home. This can be a lonely experience, so parents are allowed to be with them during the day. Parents of very ill children can even stay overnight.

The first hour of the day is often the busiest, when breakfast is served and medications are taken. Then a group of doctors, assistants, students and nurses arrive for the daily ward rounds. They visit and examine each child in turn, ask questions, talk to the nurses and make notes. The round can take two or more hours.

When the round is over, children well enough to leave their beds do so. Those under five go to a playroom where they can paint, make things, dress up and play with toys.

▶ This thermometer measures the body's temperature through the ear. It is used to take the temperature of babies and children.

Children over five may go to the schoolroom. When they are well enough to go back to school, they will be able to catch up quickly with their work.

Children who are recovering from an operation, or who have broken bones, are given exercises to strengthen their muscles. Those with chest conditions, such as asthma, are taught how to use inhalers which help their breathing.

⚠ Traction is a process of using weights to pull gently on the body. In the case of a broken leg, traction makes sure the bones are lined up so they will heal correctly. It also stretches leg muscles to stop them from shrinking through lack of use.

Traction weights

Maternity

Most babies are born in the hospital, in the maternity or labor and delivery unit.

Babies are born in the delivery room. To help reduce pain during the birth, the mother can be given a mixture of gas and air to breathe, or an injection.

As soon as a newborn baby's umbilical cord is cut, the baby starts to lead a life of its own. The nurse checks the baby to see that it is all right, then hands it to its mother for the first time.

After a few minutes the nurse cleans and weighs the baby. A soft plastic band, showing the baby's name and date of birth is fastened around the baby's wrist or ankle.

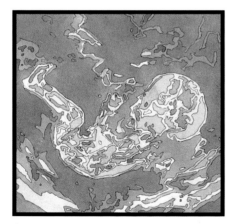

An ultrasound scan is an image of an unborn baby inside its mother. It shows whether the baby is growing normally.

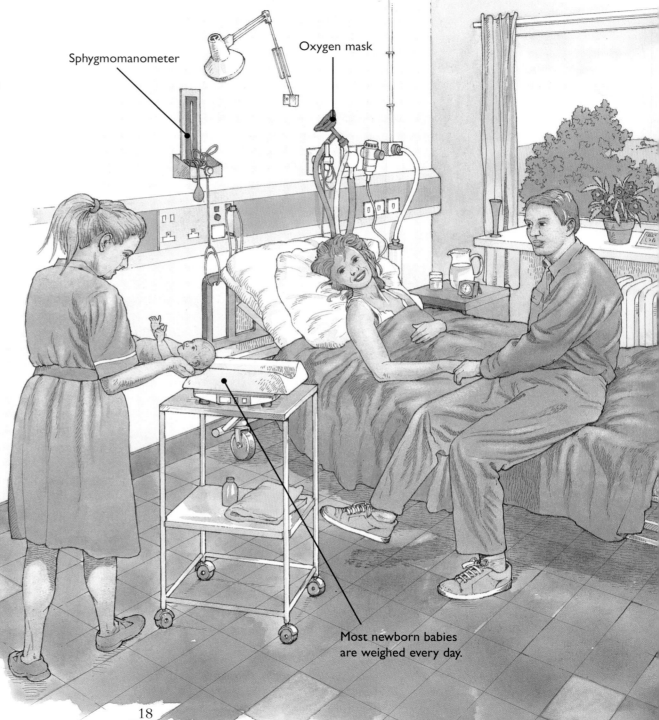

Sphygmomanometer

Oxygen mask

Most newborn babies are weighed every day.

○ A short tube—called a Pinnard stethoscope—is used by a nurse to listen to an unborn baby's heartbeat.

Back on the maternity floor, the newborn baby lies in a crib next to its mother's bed. If all is well, mother and baby can go home within a few hours of the birth.

Babies born too soon, or babies who have problems after being born, are taken to the neonatal baby unit. This is an intensive care unit just for babies, where nurses give round-the-clock care until the newborn patients are well enough to leave. This can last from just a few hours to many months.

Security is important on the maternity floor. Babies may wear electronic tags which prevent them being taken from the floor without permission. The doors are kept locked, and visitors are only let in by a member of the staff.

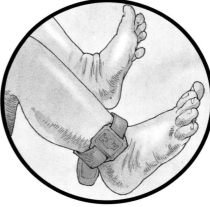

○ Many hospitals fit electronic tags to babies' ankles while they are in the maternity unit. If they are taken from the floor without permission, an alarm is sounded.

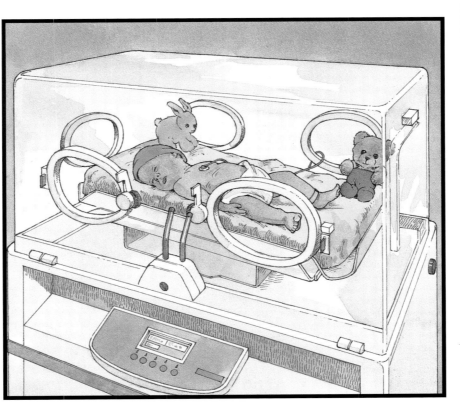

◁ A sick baby in the neonatal unit lies in an incubator. The temperature inside is carefully controlled. When the baby is well enough, it can go home, or it might need to go to the pediatric floor for further treatment.

Radiology

The radiology department has machines that look into a patient's body and take pictures of what they see. The machines use x-rays, which are invisible beams of radioactive particles.

A patient with a broken bone comes to radiology for an x-ray. In most cases the patient is sent from the emergency room. A machine directs x-rays at the break. The rays pass straight through flesh and skin. Some hard materials, such as bone and teeth, do not allow x-rays through. Rays that pass through the body hit a piece of photographic film, called a plate. When the plate is developed, bones and teeth appear as white areas. A nurse uses the x-ray to decide what type of plaster cast to apply to the break.

X-rays cannot pass through this lead safety screen.

The bed slides into position under the x-ray unit.

Protective screen

An x-ray technician operates the x-ray machine.

On an x-ray plate, bones appear white. This is a negative image. Unused plates are kept in a lead-lined box to prevent harmful radiation rays from spoiling them.

Other types of x-ray take images of the internal organs, such as the liver, stomach, kidneys or bladder. The patient is injected with a white, creamy fluid called barium sulphate—or they swallow it with food. This chemical blocks the x-rays, so the soft body tissue shows on the photographic plate. The chemical is harmless, and the body removes it naturally within a few hours.

A computerized tomography (CT) scanner uses x-rays to scan the body from all angles. It takes images of soft tissues, such as the brain. The images appear on a computer screen, from which a print out can be made. A CT scan shows a thin cross section, or slice, through the body.

High doses of x-rays damage body cells. But they can also treat cancers. Powerful x-rays kill the cells in a cancer tumor. X-ray treatment for cancer is called radiation therapy.

Computerized tomography (CT) scanner

Bed slides into the CT scanner.

⬤ Sometimes radiology technicians have to wear heavy aprons lined with lead. These protect them from the radiation put out by the x-ray machines.

Protective screen

⬤ Cross-sections through the brain made by a CT scanner. Each scan is a 2 mm-thin slice of the brain.

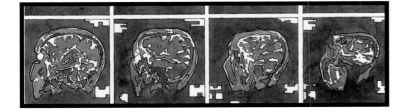

Pathology

Blood and tissue samples are examined in the pathology laboratory. It is a large department with several different sections, including the blood bank.

Blood given by donors is kept in the blood bank. It is stored in plastic bags inside refrigerated cabinets, ready to be supplied to other departments.

To examine blood, a drop is placed on a glass slide and viewed under a microscope. Individual cells can be magnified up to 500 times, making them easy to see. A scientist looks for signs of disease or infection, and checks which blood group the patient belongs to. The main blood groups are A, B, AB and O. If a patient needs blood from the bank, it must come from the same group as their own.

Laboratory staff also check a patient's health by examining bacteria found inside the body. For example, a patient may have a throat infection. Before treatment, the pathology staff have to find out the cause of the infection. A sample taken from the infected area is smeared over a layer of special gel inside a glass dish. The dish is kept at body temperature (98.6° fahrenheit) in an incubator for 24 hours. Then the microorganisms that have grown on the gel are examined. The laboratory scientist identifies the germs, and the patient is treated with the correct medications.

In another section of pathology, ultra-thin slices of tissue taken from a patient's body are prepared for examination. The tissue is stained with colored dyes to make it easier to see, then mounted on a glass slide. A scientist analyzes the slide under a microscope to find out what is wrong with the patient.

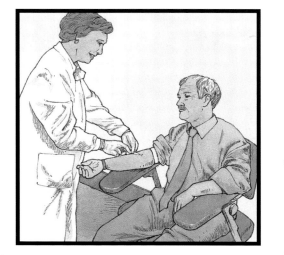

◯ A blood sample being taken from a patient's arm. Tests are performed on the blood to find out what group it belongs to and check which substances it contains.

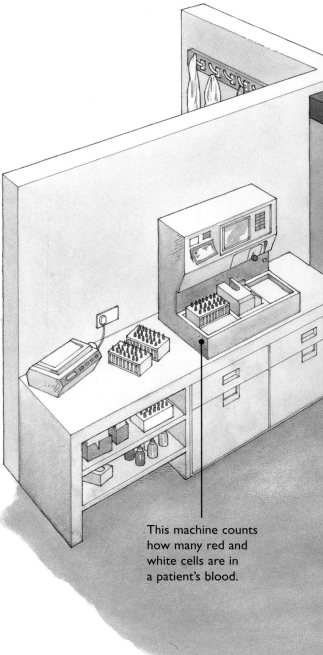

This machine counts how many red and white cells are in a patient's blood.

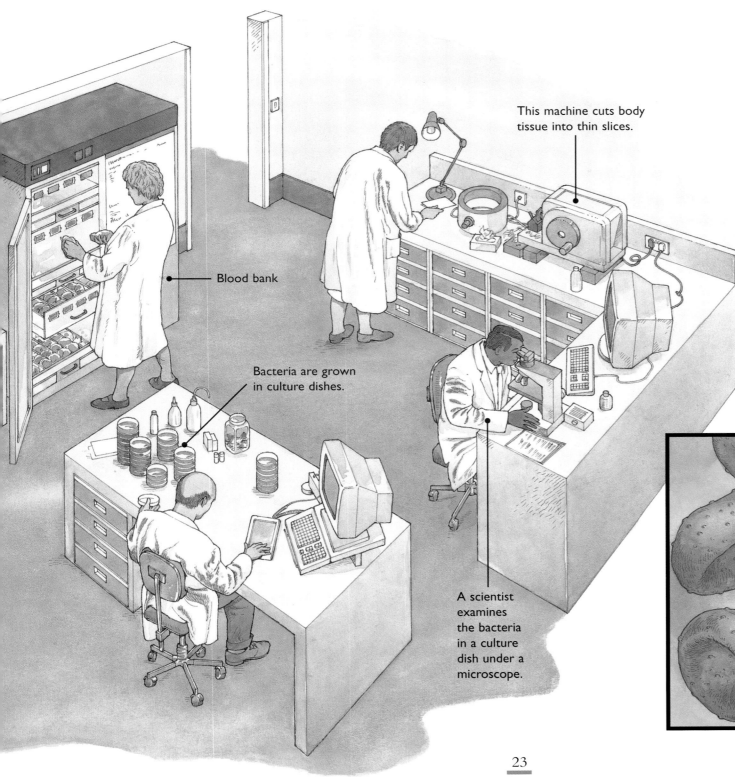

This machine cuts body tissue into thin slices.

Blood bank

Bacteria are grown in culture dishes.

A scientist examines the bacteria in a culture dish under a microscope.

Red blood cells carry oxygen around the body. Each one is about 0.025 mm across, and a blood spot the size of a pinhead contains about five million of them. A machine in pathology counts how many red cells are in a patient's blood.

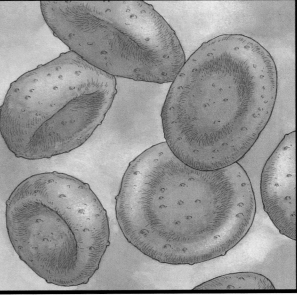

Food service and Laundry

The food service and laundry departments are in the basement of the hospital. This allows delivery vehicles to bring things straight to their doors every day.

Each morning, a patient selects their meals from the day's menu. The catering staff then decides how many different meals to prepare for the day.

Some patients are on special diets. For example, some cannot eat fat or sugar, so special meals are cooked for them.

All food is cooked fresh each day in large ovens. The temperature of cooked food is taken with a probe thermometer, to ensure it has been cooked to a high enough temperature all the way through. Microwaves are not used because of the risk they will not cook food through to the middle.

Raw food, such as salad, is kept in a refrigerator, where it is too cold for harmful germs to grow and infect it.

Meals are cooked in large ovens.

Food is kept hot inside heated serving carts.

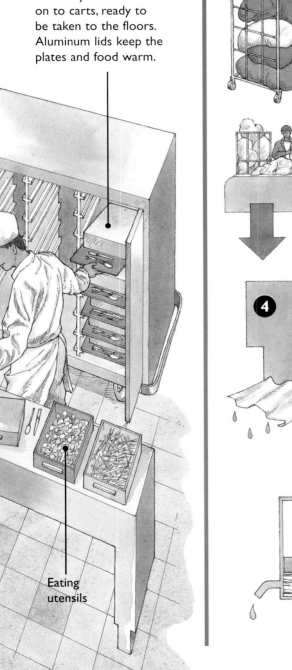

Meal trays are loaded on to carts, ready to be taken to the floors. Aluminum lids keep the plates and food warm.

Eating utensils

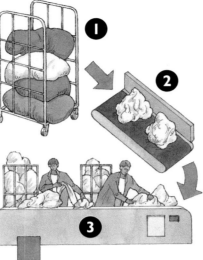

Laundry

Throughout the day, bags of dirty clothes, sheets, pillow cases, towels, blankets, uniforms and surgical gowns arrive at the laundry (1). The bags are opened (2) and the washing is sorted (3). Then it is loaded into a computer-controlled washing machine which can be set to wash at different temperatures and with different types of detergent, bleach and fabric softener (4).

A press squeezes as much moisture out of the wet laundry as possible (5) before it is put into a large tumble dryer. When the clothes are dry, they are collected in baskets (6). Flat items such as sheets and pillow cases go to an ironing machine (7), which irons and folds at the same time (8). Gowns and uniforms are dried completely and put through a folding machine which takes out the creases.

It is a non-stop cycle—as fast as cleaned items are sent back to the hospital departments, dirty items arrive here to be washed.

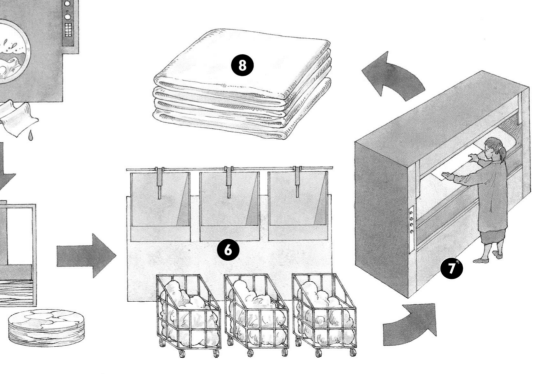

Hospital history

230s BC
Emperor Asoka of India
builds hospitals in Hindustan.

500s AD
The hospital of St.
Benedict is founded
at Monte Cassino,
a monastery in Italy.

1123
Britain's oldest hospital,
St. Bartholomew's, is
founded in London.

1719
The Westminster
Hospital opens in
London. It is one of
the first voluntary
hospitals, which
are run by town
authorities instead
of religious orders.

430s BC
Hospitals built in
Sri Lanka by Hindus.

372 AD
The Hospital of St. Basil
opens at Caesarea, Israel.
It treats the poor, the sick,
the elderly, and those
suffering from leprosy.

1099
At the time of the Crusades,
the Knights Hospitallers
of the Order of St. John
build a large hospital in
Jerusalem. Their order
exists today as the St.
John Ambulance Brigade.

100s BC
The Romans build
hospitals for the
treatment of
sick soldiers.

660 AD
A monastery hospital, the Hôtel-Dieu,
is opened in Paris, France (see page 28).
The Hôtel-Dieu is probably the world's
oldest hospital, because there has now
been a hospital on the site for more
than 1300 years.

1524
The hospital of Jesus
of Nazareth, Mexico
City, becomes the
first hospital in
North America.

1802
The world's first hospital for sick children, the Hôpital des Enfants Malades, opens in Paris.

1928
At Boston Children's Hospital in the USA, an iron lung is used for the first time. This early ventilator machine helped patients to breathe.

1978
The world's first test-tube baby is born, at Oldham District General Hospital in England.

1751
The Pennsylvania Hospital, built in Philadelphia, becomes the first US hospital.

1914
Blood from a donor is given to a patient at the Hôpital Saint-Jean in Brussels, Belgium. This is the first time blood has been successfully stored for some time before being used. It leads to the creation of blood banks.

1967
The world's first heart transplant is performed at Groote Schuur Hospital in Cape Town, South Africa. By the late 1990s, more than 2000 heart transplants are being performed in the USA every year.

1880s
The first modern operating rooms are built, made possible by the discoveries of ether (to send patients to sleep) and antiseptic sprays (to prevent infection).

1952
The world's first artificial heart is fitted to a patient for a short time at Pennsylvania Hospital in Philadelphia, USA.

1998
In a pioneering operation at the Hôpital Edouard Herriot in Lyon, France, a man has a new forearm and hand transplanted on to his right upper arm.

Changing hospitals

The hospital described in this book is a modern hospital, whose departments treat common diseases and injuries. There are many other types of hospitals, which treat specific problems or work in particular situations.

Modern hospitals can trace their origins back to the religious hospitals of the Middle Ages. Monks and nuns cared for patients as best they could, giving them medicines made from herbs and minerals, and performing simple operations. With each century that passed came new discoveries about how the body worked and how to treat disease. By the 1800s, hospitals as we know them today had arrived in towns and cities the world over.

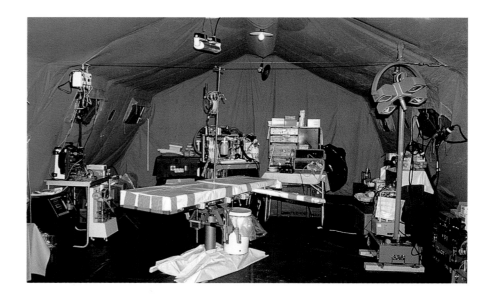

⬥ On a battlefield in the Persian Gulf, a field hospital works from inside a tent. It can be easily taken down and set up somewhere else.

⬥ This painting shows a ward in the Hôtel-Dieu hospital in Paris, about 600 years ago. The patients were cared for by nuns and often shared beds.

Specialist hospitals

These hospitals treat certain parts of the body or specific diseases only. For example, an ophthalmic hospital specializes in diseases and injuries of the eye, and an orthopedic hospital helps patients with bone problems. Patients with cancer may go to a hospital that treats this one disease, and children who need special care may go to a pediatric hospital, which is for children only. Injuries and diseases of the head and brain are treated in a neurology hospital, and mental illnesses in a psychiatric hospital.

Military hospitals

The Army, Navy and Air Force have their own specialized hospitals to treat members of the armed services. In a conflict temporary hospitals (called field hospitals) can be set up close to a battle site. Field surgeons and nurses give immediate treatment to casualties. They perform vital operations and save lives before the injured can be transferred to a larger, permanent hospital away from the war zone.

Aid hospitals

After a disaster, such as a war, earthquake, flood, fire or famine many people need medical help quickly. The Red Cross is one of the international organizations equipped to send rapid response teams to any country in need of urgent medical help. Today it is involved in projects in more than 50 countries, offering a lifeline to people who may otherwise go without medical help.

◀ A Red Cross aid hospital in Cambodia, offering food and medicine to refugees.

The 21st century

New technology will play a big part in shaping the hospitals of the future. Surgeons will practice difficult operations with the help of virtual-reality models. There may be new departments where human bodies are rebuilt after accidents. Replacing damaged limbs and organs, regenerating bone, and growing artificial skin will be as familiar as radiology and physical therapy.

▼ Telemedicine is already a reality. Here, a doctor views a brain scan taken from a patient hundreds of miles away.

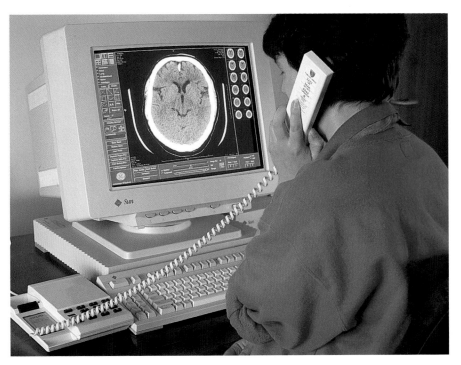

Glossary

acupuncture A Chinese healing method that works by putting fine needles into certain points of the body.

adenoids A lump of tissue at the back of the throat. It can become swollen in children, making it difficult to breathe.

allergy A reaction to a substance called an allergen. Nuts, seafood, milk, wheat, pollen, cats, dogs, house dust and mites are the most common causes of allergies.

anesthetic A mixture of drugs or gasses which send a patient into a deep sleep and stop them from moving or feeling pain during an operation.

apron An garment worn by a radiology technician that protects the upper part of the body. Some are lined with lead to prevent x-rays from reaching the body.

bacteria Microscopic organisms made up of only one cell. They were one of the first life forms to appear on Earth. Bacteria that cause diseases are often called germs.

blood bank A carefully controlled environment which stores blood given by donors. The name was first used in the USA in the 1930s.

blood pressure The pressure inside the body's blood vessels. It varies with age and health.

computerized tomography (CT) A method of examining the body that uses x-rays to make detailed pictures of the internal organs.

crash cart Another name for a resuscitation cart. It contains everything needed in an emergency, such as medication, needles, feeding and breathing tubes.

culture dish A transparent plastic or glass dish in which scientists grow bacteria under controlled conditions. It can also be called a Petri dish.

defibrillator A machine that gives a patient an electric shock to restart or improve the beat of the heart.

diabetes A disease where the body is unable to control the level of sugar in the blood. It can be controlled but not cured.

dose The amount of medicine a patient is given.

ear tube A small ring made of plastic or rubber. Some people have them placed inside the ear to improve hearing.

ether A colorless chemical, used as the first anesthetic in 1846 by an American dentist, William Morton.

hospital A place where sick people receive treatment for their conditions. The words hospital, hotel, and hostel all come from the Latin word *hospitalis*, meaning hospitable.

hydrotherapy A method of healing a patient using water.

incubator A transparent container for a sick baby that holds air at body temperature (98.6° fahrenheit).

isolator A machine in which certain medicines and liquid foods are prepared without coming into contact with anything which may contaminate them.

kidney stones A painful condition caused by hard lumps forming in the kidneys. A minor operation is needed to remove them.

leprosy A disease of the skin and nerves which used to be common around the world. Today leprosy is only found in countries close to the equator.

life support machine Any machine which supports the body's normal functions, such as breathing or removing waste.

microorganism A living thing which is too small to see with the naked eye.

microscope An instrument for seeing tiny objects close up.

morgue A building where dead bodies are kept before burial or cremation.

obstetric nurse A person who is trained to help during childbirth.

ophthalmology unit A department where eye disorders are treated.

outpatient A patient who needs hospital treatment, but who is well enough to stay at home.

pediatrics The study of children's health.

paramedic A person who is trained to give immediate help at the scene of an accident.

Pascal's triangle A measuring tray for counting loose tablets.

pharmacist A person who is trained to prepare and give, or dispense medicine.

physical therapist A person who is trained to help patients recover the use of their body's mobility after an accident, an illness or an operation.

prescription Instructions written by a doctor which describe the medicine a patient is to be given.

psychiatry A department for the treatment of mental illnesses.

radiologist A person who is trained to work with x-rays.

radiology A method of examining the inner parts of the body with x-rays.

rounds The daily visit by a doctor to the patients on a floor.

sphygmomanometer An instrument for measuring blood pressure.

sterile Not contaminated by germs.

stethoscope An instrument used to hear sounds made by the heart and lungs.

stitches Thread which joins together the edges of a wound.

surgeon A member of the medical staff who specializes in performing operations.

telemedicine Using computers and video links to send medical information between hospitals that may be thousands of miles apart. It saves having to move patients between hospitals.

telemetry transmitter A device worn by a patient which transmits signals to a computer, keeping nurses aware of the patient's condition.

thermometer An instrument for measuring the temperature of a patient's body.

traction A means of treatment that uses weights to gently pull on the body.

triage From a French word meaning "sorting according to condition," where patients are quickly assessed to decide how urgent their treatment should be.

ultrasound A method of examining parts of the body using sound waves. Images are shown on a screen, from which print outs can be made.

umbilical cord The fleshy tube that connects an unborn baby to its mother. The cord is cut when the baby is born, leaving the navel or belly button.

ventilator A machine that moves air into and out of a patient's lungs to keep them breathing.

vital signs A patient's life signs. Heart rate, blood pressure, breathing rate, and the amount of oxygen in the blood are the most important signs which are checked regularly.

x-rays A form of radiation that passes through the soft tissues of the body. They are used in radiology.

Index

Published in the United States in 1999 by
Peter Bedrick Books
A division of NTC/Contemporary Publishing Group, Inc.
4255 West Touhy Avenue
Lincolnwood (Chicago), Illinois 60646-1975, U.S.A.

Copyright © Belitha Press Limited 1999
Text copyright © John Malam 1999

Hospital cutaway illustrations: David Cuzik
All other illustrations: William Donohoe
Series editor: Mary-Jane Wilkins
Editor: Russell Mclean
Designer: Guy Callaby
Picture researcher: Diana Morris
Consultant: Susan Francis
Series concept: Christine Hatt

If you would like to comment on this book,
write to the author at johnmalam@aol.com

The author and publishers wish to thank the staff of Mid Cheshire
Hospitals NHS Trust at Leighton Hospital, Crewe, who kindly
allowed access to the departments described in this book.

Library of Congress Cataloging-in-Publication Data
Malam, John.
    Hospital / John Malam.
      p.   cm. — (Building works)
    Summary: Reveals the inner workings of a typical modern
    general hospital by exploring the various departments, other
    key places, the equipment, the employees, and what takes place
    there.
      ISBN 0-87226-585-4 (hc)
      1. Hospitals Juvenile literature.   2. Hospital care Juvenile
    literature.   [1. Hospitals.   2. Medical care.]   I. Title.
    II. Series.
    RA963.5.M34   1999
    362.1'1—dc21   99-24757
                                                          CIP

Printed and Bound in China

International Standard Book Number: 0-87226-585-4

99 00 01 02 03 15 14 13 12 11 10 9 8 7 6 5 4 3 2 1

Picture acknowledgements: Simon Fraser/SPL: 28br.
FSP/Gamma/ECPA: 27tr. Teit Hornbak/Still Pictures: 28 left.
Wellcome Trust Library, London: 27bl.

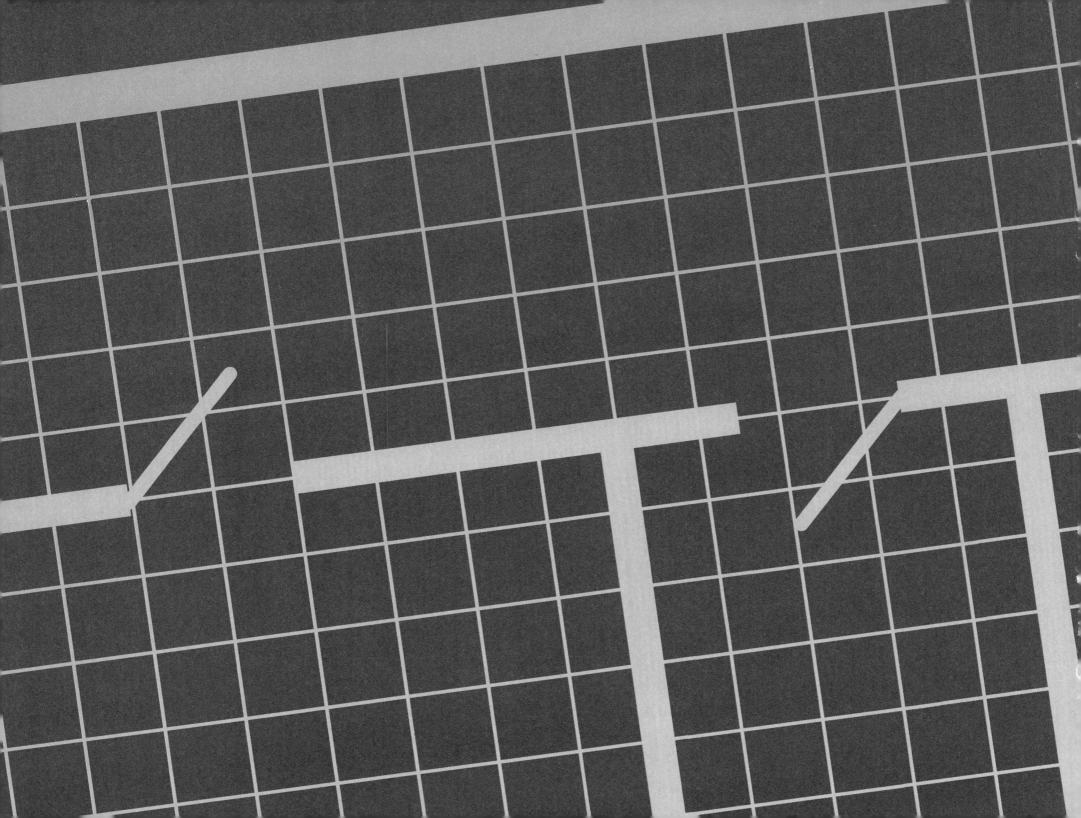